The Culper Ring: The History and Legacy of the Revolutionary War's Most Famous Spy Ring

By Charles River Editors

A page from the Culper Ring's codebook

About Charles River Editors

Charles River Editors provides superior editing and original writing services across the digital publishing industry, with the expertise to create digital content for publishers across a vast range of subject matter. In addition to providing original digital content for third party publishers, we also republish civilization's greatest literary works, bringing them to new generations of readers via ebooks.

Sign up here to receive updates about free books as we publish them, and visit Our Kindle Author Page to browse today's free promotions and our most recently published Kindle titles.

Introduction

A depiction of British ships in New York Harbor

The Culper Ring

After the siege of Boston forced the British to evacuate that city in March 1776, Continental Army commander George Washington suspected that the British would move by sea to New York City, the next logical target in an attempt to end a colonial insurrection. He thus rushed his army south to defend the city.

Washington guessed correctly, but it would be to no avail. Unlike Boston, New York City's terrain featured few defensible positions. The city lacked a high point from which to launch a siege, as the peninsula of Boston was fortunate to have. Moreover, Washington wasn't sure defending the city was necessary, hoping that an expedition launched toward Quebec like the one Benedict Arnold had led in late 1775 would keep the British away from New York anyway. However, Congress thought otherwise, and demanded that Washington defend New York.

Washington thus did what he was told, and it nearly resulted in the army's demise. In the summer of 1776, the British conducted the largest amphibious expedition in North America's history at the time, landing over 20,000 troops on Long Island. British General William Howe, who had led the British at Bunker Hill and would later become commander in chief of the armies in North America, easily captured Staten Island, which Washington was incapable of defending without a proper navy. Washington's army attempted to fight, but Washington was badly outmaneuvered, and his army was nearly cut off from escape. The withdrawal across New York City was enormously disorderly, with many of Washington's troops so scared that they deserted. Others were sick as a result of the dysentery and smallpox plaguing the Continental Army in New York. In what was arguably the worst defeat of the Revolution, Washington was ashamed, and he also felt betrayed, by both his troops and Congress.

To escape from New York, Washington led a tactical retreat across the East River and off Long Island in the middle of the night without British knowledge. This retreat prevented the annihilation of the colonial army in New York, but with Washington being pushed west across New Jersey and into Pennsylvania, Congress was forced to flee Philadelphia. And with this string of crucial British successes in 1776, the Revolution was on the brink of failure.

However, unbeknownst to nearly everyone, Washington had some men remain active in New York City: the now famous Culper Ring, one of the Revolution's first major intelligence efforts. The ring consisted mostly of a group of civilians in and around New York City who spied on the British forces and Loyalist Americans and reported what they saw and overheard ultimately to Washington, who took a personal, hands-on approach to their management. After modern histories brought their story more fully to light, these spies have since become the subject (with the historical facts somewhat altered) of a recent hit television show, *Turn: Washington's Spies*.

Without question, the relatively little-known clandestine actions of these patriotic men and women contributed to the eventual victory of the long struggle for American independence, and several good books cover part or all of the history of the Culper Ring. However, the main sources consist of the correspondence, much of which has somehow survived, between the members of the ring and their military handlers. Like other spy tales, theirs is a story of courage fraught with constant suspense at being found out and facing a caught spy's usual fate of imprisonment and execution. Indeed, around the time the ring was being organized, America's most famous spy, Nathan Hale, had been caught with maps of British positions on Long Island in his possession and had been summarily hanged.

The Culper Ring: The History and Legacy of the Revolutionary War's Most Famous Spy Ring profiles the members of the ring and their activities. Along with pictures of important people, places, and events, you will learn about the Culper Ring like never before, in no time at all.

The Culper Ring: The History and Legacy of the Revolutionary War's Most Famous Spy Ring

About Charles River Editors

Introduction

Chapter 1: The Historical Context

21st century spy satellites are more than capable of photographing automobile license plates and street addresses on the ground from several hundred miles high up in earth orbit. More importantly for the military, they can provide all kinds of useful details about the size and disposition of an enemy's forces. In the early 1960s, high-altitude U2 spy plane flights were able to detect and photograph Soviet missiles sites under construction in Cuba and take photos as telling evidence. During the U.S. Civil War (1860-65), hydrogen gas and hot-air balloons were employed by both the Union and the Confederates to take a peek from 1000 feet at what the other side was up to on the battlefield. The first use of balloons for military surveillance purposes occurred in 1794 during the wars of the French Revolution, not long after balloons that could carry human passengers were invented. During the American Revolution (1775-81), commanding officers did not have any aerial option. They were totally dependent upon the intelligence that human spies operating at ground level could collect and send through hand-written dispatches to headquarters, and they made widespread use of such espionage methods.

George Washington was well-aware of the necessity of having good intelligence. During the French & Indian War, he had been present in 1755 when British Gen. Braddock's expeditionary force of redcoats had fallen into a trap and been annihilated by a French and Indian ambush. Washington then had to shoulder the task of leading the ragged retreat of the survivors home to Virginia. When Washington took command of the Continental Army at the siege of Boston in 1775, spies from within the British lines brought out useful information. The British also had their own set of agents operating in the rebel-held countryside. When the British left Boston in March 1776 and transferred their main locus of operations in North American to suppress the colonial rebellion to the more central location of New York City, Washington found himself largely in the blind about the intentions and movements of the British army and navy. Driven off of Long Island and out of Manhattan and Westchester County and forced to withdraw to eastern Pennsylvania with the demoralized remnants of his army, Washington was able to make a successful, morale-building surprise Christmas attack on the unsuspecting enemy at Trenton, New Jersey, because, for a change, he did have good, actionable intelligence from a civilian supporter who had visited the Hessian garrison under the guise of carrying on some trade.

Washington

After capturing and occupying New York City as their main base of operations, the next major campaign launched by the British was to take the rebel capital of Philadelphia. This they accomplished in September 1777, after battling Washington's outnumbered and less well-trained Continentals and patriot militias. (Washington planted spies in Philadelphia before pulling out to remain at a safe, watchful distance from the countryside.) In June 1778, the British departed

Philadelphia and returned their occupying forces to New York. Here they remained ensconced until the end of the war in 1783. New York City and Long Island already had a fair number of Loyalists, and numerous additional "Tories" fled to the city as refugees. In the rural hinterlands around the city, a low-intensity warfare took place that also involved not only the British but also units of American Loyalists fighting against other Americans who favored independence.

Washington established his headquarters in New Jersey and later in the Hudson Highlands. With the patriot side now supported by the might of the French Crown, he wanted to attack and liberate the city if he could find a way to exploit some weaknesses on the part of the enemy occupiers. For this to have any chance of success, he required good, solid intelligence which had been largely lacking in 1776 when the fighting had taken place previously around the city. It was in this context that the Culper Ring began its clandestine operations in the summer of 1778.

Chapter 2: People and Places

Washington's chief handler of the Culper Ring for the duration of its operations from 1778 to 1783 was Major Benjamin Tallmadge. Tallmadge came from the Long Island town of Setauket. Son of the town's Presbyterian minister, Tallmadge had graduated from Yale in 1773. Then, fired with patriotic spirit, he had been commissioned as an officer in the 2nd Continental Light Dragoons in 1776 and saw action around Philadelphia. In as much as Tallmadge had grown up in Setauket and thus had many friends and acquaintances there, it made sense, when asked by Washington to take on the intelligence job, to cultivate an operation that was centered there.

Tallmadge

The village of Setauket, part of the town of Brookhaven, faced the patriot-held southern shore of Connecticut a dozen miles across Long Island Sound. It had been founded in 1655 by Puritan settlers from New England. Given this cultural and religious background, it was not surprising that a good many of the Setauket townsfolk were pro-independence, but they could not be too outspoken about their sympathies because other residents of the village and its surrounding towns were committed Loyalists and the village was occupied part of the time by a detachment of Loyalist soldiers. Setauket's sheltered harbor made the village important to the British as a place from which cordwood needed for cooking and keeping warm could be shipped to the city. The Loyalist garrison in Setauket was attacked in August 1777 by a force of Continentals who crossed the Sound. However, intelligence of their plans had leaked out enabling the Loyalist defenders to fortify heavily, and the attackers had returned to Connecticut after only a brief exchange of fire. Although more than 50 miles as the crow flies from Manhattan where the British center of operations was located, Setauket was connected to the city by a road along the shore of the Sound along which agricultural goods and merchandise often passed -- providing a good cover for patriot spies to transmit their information back and forth undetected.

Abraham Woodhull was the principal espionage agent on the scene in Setauket who was recruited by Tallmadge. At the time of the Revolution, Woodhull was unmarried and working his farm with the aid of his slaves. Abraham's uncle, John Woodhull, was one of the main Brookhaven patriot leaders having signed the 1775 revolutionary Associators Oath and acted in May 1776 as the chair of a committee formed to institute proceedings against local Tories. Another uncle, Nathan Woodhull, John's younger brother and a Setauket merchant, was a captain in the Continental Army. Abraham was also a distant cousin of Gen. Nathaniel Woodhull, a highly-regarded veteran of the French & Indian War, who, in a major loss for the patriots, was captured by the British while helping to defend Long Island from the enemy invasion and succumbed from his wounds and cruel British prison ship treatment in September 1776. On the other hand, Abraham's father, Richard Woodhull, had been a colonial judge and seems to have taken a more pragmatic position with regards to declaring loyalties in the conflict.

A contemporary depiction of Nathaniel Woodhull's capture

Caleb Brewster, the son of a Setauket farmer, played an essential role because of his intimate knowledge of Long Island geography on land and sea. Before the Revolution, he had gone to sea and then joined the Continental Army. Using his sailing experience, Lt. later Capt. Brewster ran whale boats back and forth from across Long Island Sound avoiding the British and Loyalist patrols while sometimes harassing them and transferring information gathered in Setauket to his old friend Benjamin Tallmadge in Connecticut. This information then eventually made its way by horseback to Gen. Washington, wherever he and his command happened to be located.

Anna Strong – sometimes called "Nancy" -- was the wife of Selah Strong, a Setauket militia captain and delegate to the New York provincial congresses who had been imprisoned by the British. She lived with her eight children in a cottage on their farm while the main house was occupied by Loyalist officers. According to a story handed-down in the Strong family that is perhaps apocryphal but nevertheless a good one, Anna used her clothes line to enable the spies to make contact with each other. A black petticoat – black being an unusual color for items of female intimate attire at that time – was a sign for Abraham Woodhull, who lived on the opposite side of Setauket's Little Bay from the Strong family cottage, that Brewster had arrived from Connecticut, and the number of white handkerchief hung out on the line to dry indicated which one of six coves was where Brewster was awaiting Woodhull to receive his spy reports.

Austin Roe was a Setauket resident and tavern owner who carried messages by horseback to and from the spy ring's operatives in New York City. He used a clever method to transfer information. He owned cows that shared a field with Woodhull's cows which gave Roe an opportunity and a good cover to leave and retrieve messages in a box hidden in the field's brush.

New York City at the time of the Revolution was much smaller territorially than it is today. Only the lower portion of Manhattan Island was marked off into a grid of streets from the Battery north to the vicinity of Delancey Street with houses, churches, shops and other structures. The remainder of Manhattan consisted of scattered farmsteads and meadow lands having only two small villages, Greenwich Village and Harlem. New York's population was 25,000, which made it the second largest city in the colonies behind Philadelphia's 40,000, and shortly after the British takeover in September 1776, a fire of unknown origins broke out in the city and, picked up by high winds, spread rapidly from there. Before it was done burning, the fire had consumed fully a quarter of the city's crowded-together houses and buildings. Along with the British troops, the city was packed full of Loyalist refugees from the countryside.

Robert Townsend was the ring's main intelligence agent in New York City. Townsend operated a profitable grocery and dry goods business in the city and was a silent partner in a popular coffee house, both of which put him into frequent contact with British soldiers and officers and Loyalist personages. He was not suspected of disloyalty by the British because he was a Quaker, most of whom, as pacifists, were taking a neutral stance towards the war. The fact that Townsend's family home was located at Oyster Bay on the Sound some 25 miles west of Setauket gave him an excellent cover for undertaking trips between the city and Long Island. Robert's father, Samuel, had been a member of the Provincial Congress and the Committee of Safety and had helped to provision the revolutionary army defending Long Island from the British. However, after the British drove out Washington's men, he had elected to take the Oath of Allegiance to the Crown and, like many others, had British officers quartering in his house.

Robert Townsend

A contemporary sketch of Townsend

The historic Oyster Bay home of Robert Townsend, now a museum

It seems Robert Townsend was driven to embrace the patriot cause and become a spy due to his anger at abuse British soldiers had administered to his family and from being persuaded of the justice of the cause through reading Tom Paine's *Common Sense*. Townsend and Abraham Woodhull became acquainted because Townsend sometimes roomed at the boardinghouse that was run in the city by Woodhull's sister Mary and her husband, Amos Underhill. Underhill, who was probably aware of the spy ring's existence, happened to be a cousin of Townsend's. At some point while they were sharing the same room and board, Woodhull recruited Townsend.

James Rivington was the other principal Culper Ring spy for the patriots located in the city. Rivington was totally trusted by the enemy as the publisher of a rabidly pro-British newspaper and, as such, was an extraordinary source of valuable information. Rivington was also Townsend's partner in the coffee house business, and this is probably how Townsend was able to recruit him. When and why Rivington decided to become a spy for those he was lambasting in print is not clear. The best guess is that he decided to switch sides in 1778 after the major British military failures for fear that he and his would family would need protection from patriot mobs if the British cut their losses and evacuated. Indeed, after the British acknowledged American independence and evacuated in 1783, he continued to live in the U.S., unlike many Loyalists who evacuated with the British to take up new lives in Canada or in Great Britain.

Rivington

The name of the "Culper Ring" came from a suggestion by Gen. Washington himself, taking the word from Culpepper County in his home state of Virginia. Washington came up with the code name for Abraham Woodhull, dubbing him "Samuel Culper. When Robert Townsend joined the ring, Woodhull became "Samuel Culper, Sr." and Townsend became "Samuel Culper, Jr." Tallmadge's pseudonym for covert written communication was "John Bolton." The members of the ring each also had use of an individual numerical code, with Washington's being "711."

Chapter 3: The Spies at Work

The story of the Culper Ring opens with the tragic capture and death of Nathan Hale in September 1776. Hale, a young officer in the Continental Army from Connecticut, had been asked by Washington to go behind British lines on Long Island and bring back information on the what the British were up to there. Hale was quickly identified by Loyalists, found with incriminating papers on his body, and executed. This abject failure due to bad luck and ineptitude convinced Washington of the need to develop a more properly-prepared body of secret service agents that could bring him the information he needed to make good military decisions. While in the Continental Army's winter quarters at Morristown, New Jersey, over the winter of 1776 to 1777, Washington began to organize what he thought would be needed.

A statue depicting Hale in New York City

A contemporary depiction of Hale's hanging

Washington's initially made a contract with Nathaniel Sackett, a Fishkill, New York merchant, to provide intelligence around the New York area. Sackett had some prior espionage experience as a member of the Committee and Commission for Detecting and Defeating Conspiracies established by New York's revolutionary legislature. In a letter written to Sackett dated February 4, 1777, Washington entrusted him with "obtaining the earliest and best Intelligence of the designs of the Enemy" and authorized the payment of $50 per month to him, along with the setting up of a fund of $500 from which Sackett could pay agents and informants. Within several weeks, Sackett through William Duer, the Continental Congressman who had recommended him, was passing Washington intelligence he had collected on the British and Loyalists. In April, Sackett provided useful information about the preparations of the British to attack Philadelphia. However, for reasons unknown, Washington soon thereafter terminated his relationship with Sackett in New York and focused on developing a intelligence network in Philadelphia. It was not until mid-1778 that a systematic intelligence effort was organized again in the New York area, as the focus of the war shifted back northward again from Philadelphia.

The first person whom Washington asked to reestablish an intelligence network around New York was Brig. Gen. Charles Scott, the commander of a Virginia brigade stationed north of the British-occupied city. When Scott was furloughed home in November 1778, Washington was in need of a new chief of intelligence and next turned to Maj. Benjamin Tallmadge. Tallmadge's position as an officer in the Continental Army's Second Light Dragoons, tasked with patrolling the Connecticut shore, provided an excellent cover for him to direct intelligence operations in New York. Directly across Long Island Sound from southern Connecticut was British and Tory-held Long Island, including Tallmadge's home town of Setauket where he knew many people.

Scott

According to one popular account which may have some credence, Tallmadge recruited his old Setauket friend or acquaintance Abraham Woodhull when Woodhull was caught shipping his farm products by water to the British in the city. Tallmadge may have helped secure Woodhull's release from imprisonment and extracted as a *quid pro quo* from Woodhull, who had been neutral in the conflict thus far, that he would act as a spy for the patriots. In any case, regardless of how Woodhull was persuaded, based on letters we find in the Washington archives,

Tallmadge seems to have procured Woodhull's services during August 1778. By mid-November, he was receiving intelligence from "Culper" and passing on instructions to him from Washington with specific questions to answer about the British military's strength and disposition. For that purpose, Woodhull began in late 1778 and throughout early 1779 making a series of seemingly innocent business trips to New York City, where he mingled with the British in the streets and at the boarding house run by his sister and brother-in-law. Then, once home in Setauket, Woodhull wrote up and reported what he had learned to Townsend, sending it through means of Caleb Brewster's boats across Long Island Sound to Connecticut. Tallmadge then passed on the information by a chain of couriers riding on horseback to Gen. Washington.

In a letter to Washington dated November 19, 1778, Tallmadge described Woodhull, whose identity Washington never knew, as being extremely cautious and timid and unwilling to let his identify be known to anyone else but himself. Indeed, it was not until after the Revolution was over that Woodhull's activities became much known, and he never wrote anything about them himself. In a memoir about his Revolutionary War experiences written in later years for his children, Tallmadge revealed only about his own espionage role that in 1778 he had "opened a private correspondence with some persons in New York [for General Washington] which lasted through the war. How beneficial it was to the Commander-in-Chief is evidenced by his continuing the same to the close of the war. I kept one or more boats continually employed in crossing the Sounds on this business. . . .My station was in the county of Westchester, and occasionally along the shores of the Sound. " That was all he ever let be known. Fortunately, much of the back-and-forth correspondence between Tallmadge and Washington, including attachments of the spies' own reports, managed to survive the war, and historians can use these letters to piece together the rudiments of this fascinating story and learn about the spy methods used.

Woodhull in his early reports, which numbered eight by March 1779, from making his trips into the city from Setauket, reported some successes to Tallmadge and Washington: He had held a conversational exchange with Maj. Gen. Tyron, the former colonial governor of New York and had made direct observations of the British Commander-in Chief Gen. Clinton. Along with providing details of British military strength and their comings and goings, Woodhull urged Washington to make a sudden attack on the city which he felt was undermanned by its defenders. Expressing hope that the war would soon be over, he wrote emotionally about how the British quartered on Long Island were abusing Americans, regardless of whether they were Whigs or Tories, by stripping the farmers' barns and outhouses of their wood to use it in building huts for the winter and by taking their cattle hay without paying. Woodhull also passed along news which he picked up in the city from conversations or by reading newspapers about political developments in European countries favorable to the American cause, which Washington was then able to share with other patriot leaders to help with maintaining morale.

Woodhull's reports made from Setauket were often disjointed and drafted with less-than-perfect grammar and syntax. In a letter to Tallmadge dated April 10, 1779, Woodhull apologized for that fact: "When ever I Sit down I always feel and know my Inability to write a good Letter. As my calling in life never required it—Nor led to consider, how necessary a qualification it was for a Man—And much less did I think it would ever fall to my lot, to Serve in Such Publick and important buisiness as this, And my letters perused by one of the worthiest Men on Earth. But I trust he will overlook any imperfections he may discover in the dress of my words—And rest assured that I indevour to collect and convey the most accurate and explicit intelligence that I possibly can, And hope it may be of Some Service towards Alleviateing the miseries of our disstressed Count[r]y. Nothing but that could have induced me to undertake it, for you must readily think, it is a life of anxiety to be within (on Such buisiness) the lines of a cruel and mistrustfull Enemy and that I most Ardently wish and impatiently wait for their departure."

Lt. Brewster, who conveyed Woodhull's reports by boat across Long Island Sound, also sometimes enclosed his own reports about British and Loyalist doings on Long Island. But Washington thought the Brewster route took too long for information to reach him. In a letter written March 21, 1779 to Maj. Tallmadge in which he enclosed 50 gold guineas for espionage use, Washington urged that a more direct route across the Hudson to deliver the information be found from the city to his present encampment in Middlebrook, New Jersey. An alternative route was sought – a route that used the services of a patriot contact on Staten Island or in Bergen, NJ – but it never materialized due to the danger involved, and the same long, circuitous route from the city out to Setauket and then across Long Island Sound to Connecticut. From there, it was sent to Washington, thus requiring several hundred miles of travel.

Washington suggested in this same letter that "Culper" consider relocating permanently to New York, where he could "mix with—and put on the airs of a Tory to cover his real character, & avoid suspicion." But Woodhull vetoed this idea, concluding that removing from Setauket would be unwise for his own safety. Moreover, Woodhull had become more and more worried that his frequent trips of New York were raising suspicions that might lead to his exposure. In Setauket, Woodhull had a near-brush with exposure in April when a Loyalist returning on parole from Connecticut imprisonment "lodged information" concerning Woodhull with Col. Simcoe of the Queen's Rangers. Simcoe raided the Woodhull residence to look for him. Fortunately, Woodhull had left the day previously for New York. However, Woodhull's father suffered abuse from the Loyalist soldiers who were angry at having missed Woodhull himself.

Woodhull had good reason to be fearful of detection from making too many trips to New York and being too inquisitive. Starting in April 1779, the British had an effective intelligence and counter-intelligence operation in and around New York run by Maj. John André . To make the secret correspondence more difficult for the enemy to find and read, Washington provided Tallmadge with a vial of invisible ink that he in turn passed on to Woodhull. Woodhull was reportedly "much pleased" to use it, although Woodhull reported he had spilled and lost much of the ink when he was surprised in his room while at work by intruders (whom he feared might be the British soldiers who quartered in his house but turned out to be his nieces playing a game on their uncle), and he had to request more. The invisible ink was also passed on to Townsend for use in writing his reports sent from New York. As an added precaution, the writing would be done in the margins or on the blank pages of a book. Or, a sheet of writing paper would be removed from a ream of paper, the report written on it with the invisible ink and then returned to the very same place in the package, a location that was known only to the recipient at the other end so that it could be extracted and the ink made visible again. The package was then carefully resealed to look as though it was untouched and then given to the post rider to be carried to Setauket in company with other goods that were being delivered. A chemical solution from a second vial that Washington provided Tallmadge for his agents was applied with a brush to the paper to make the "stain" visible. Washington insisted on the utmost degree of secrecy about the method used for fear that the British might possess something similar they could use.

André's self portrait of himself

Tallmadge came up with an additional means for rendering the correspondence more secure. In the place of locations, persons and important things, numbers could be substituted for the words in the letters. Thus, in a chart he devised for the spies' use, New York City would become "721," Setauket would be "729," and England would be "745" (the last number possibly echoing the famous 1763 English broadside, John Wilkes's "North Briton No. 45," that criticized King George III and led to a major struggle in defense of free speech). Gen. Washington was "711" while his counterpart, Gen. Clinton was "712." Samuel Culper was "722" and Culper Jr. was

"723." Hypocrite was "276," peace was "470," a Tory was "639," tyranny was "646," and so on – 763 code numbers in all, ending with a number for "headquarters." To safeguard other data, letters and numbers could be substituted for letters and numbers. Washington held his own copy of the code, and Woodhull began utilizing the code numbers in his reports in early June.

The addition of a new spy to the ring, this spy a resident in the city and thus much better-positioned than Woodhull, who had to travel back and forth from Setauket, to acquire useful information, is first mentioned in Woodhull's No. 14 on June 24th. Woodhull announced that he had "comunicatied my buisiness to an Intimate freind. And disclosed every Secret and laid before him every instruction that hath bene handed to me." With great difficulty due to the person's fear, he had gained the person's compliance and was assured that he was "a Person that hath the Intrest of our Country at heart and of good reputation Charecter and family as any of my Acquaintance." Woodhull stressed that this persons's identity could never be revealed to anyone but to the post rider conveying the messages who unavoidably must know who he was. "I have reason to think his advantages for Serving you and Abilityties are far Superior to mine."

As we know now, the person in question was the New York-based merchant Robert Townsend, who had roomed at Woodhull's sister's and brother-in-law's boarding house who Woodhull said he had thus known for several years. By July, Washington was receiving weekly reports from this pseudonymous "Samuel Culper, Jr," and he remained a valued source along with "Samuel Culper, Sr. during the rest of the conflict. Townsend as a businessman was a more skillful, even elegant letter writer than Woodhull. The potential value of Townsend's information began to be shown early on when he disclosed the identity of a former New York City patriot leader who was now living in exile in Connecticut but acting as an agent for David Mathews, the Tory mayor of New York. Townsend subsequently recruited the newspaperman, James Rivington, who was even better positioned to acquire intelligence because he was an outspoken Loyalist who consorted freely with many high-ranking members of the British military and government.

The importance of maintaining a high level of security with use of a code was made evident in early July when a body of British cavalry and infantry crossed over the Sound under cover of darkness and attacked the encampment where Tallmadge was located. During the hasty retreat the Continentals were forced to beat, Tallmadge had lost his horse and his field baggage which contained letters and money from Washington destined for the spies. An embarrassed Tallmadge had to notify Washington, ask for a replacement of the money that had been lost, and hear a chastisement from his superior about keeping any important papers at an advanced post.

Woodhull reported that he found himself in danger from Loyalist refugees who "are let loss [loose] to P[l]under within and without their lines Parties of them are hideing in the Woods and laying Wait for the unwary and Ignorant to deceive them puting on the Charecter of Peopele from your Shore and have Succeeded in there design too well, carried of[f] 10 or 12 Men and Striped their houses lately from about 20, the Roads from here to 10 [New York] is infested by them, and likewise the Shores that Maks our Corespondence very dangerous and requires great

Cair and a Strict observance of the before mentioned Charecters and circumstances that may tend to discover."

In early July 1779, as part of a plan by the British Commander-in-Chief Clinton to draw Washington into battle, British Maj. Gen. Tryon led a force of several thousand soldiers who raided and wreaked destruction on towns along the shore of Connecticut. Woodhull wrote Tallmadge that "With Sorrow [I] beheld the Smock of your Towns. And very desereous to here the event. from the report of guns it is Judged you made a desparate defence."

Along with running an important espionage network, Maj. Tallmadge kept up with his various military duties. This involved not only guarding the Connecticut shore but sometimes taking the fight to the enemy. On September 5th 1779, Tallmadge led an expeditionary force in whale boats that crossed the Sound to attack a fortified British and Loyalist military post at Lloyd's Neck, about twenty miles west of Setauket. This raid was totally successful in disrupting "a large band of marauders" who had been raiding the Connecticut coast. Tallmadge was happy to report to the Commander in Chief that he had lost not a single man in the operation. As revealed in his correspondence with Washington, Tallmadge was also engaged during this time period in the more pedestrian but essential activity of recruiting more men for the dragoons of which he was officer and of securing what his men needed in the way of uniforms, linen and provisions.

During the summer and autumn of 1779, Washington was mulling over the feasibility of an attack on the British in New York. A French fleet was arriving to take up station in North America, and the Culper Ring was reporting to him that the British troops were dispersed in smaller units and that the Tories were demoralized. Writing from his headquarters at West Point, Washington through Tallmadge issued specific instructions to the spies about gathering information that he might need for the planning and execution of an attack. Washington's questions concerned whether the British naval transports were being protected from fire rafts, the numbers of men defending the city and where they were posted, the fortifications being strengthened by the British, and the state of provisions forage and fuel "as also the Health and Spirits of the Army, Navy and City." Culper Jr. was to remain in the city "to collect all the useful information he can—to do this, he should mix as much as possible among the Officers and Refugees, visit the Coffee Houses and all public places." Culper Sr. was to stay fast at his station on Long Island and continue to fulfill his role of receiving and transmitting the information. Washington stressed the need for "the greatest Caution and secrecy in a Business so critical and dangerous" and that the information gathered was to be transmitted to nobody but himself.

Unfortunately, a many-months-long gap exists in the primary source materials from October 1779 to May 1780, when nothing much is known about the activities of the Culper Ring. During this time period, Washington decided, after weighing the pros and cons based in part on the intelligence gathered by his spies, not to launch an attack on New York City in tandem with the French. In late October, the British garrison in Newport, Rhode Island was evacuated. With those soldiers plus additional reinforcements that came in from England under Gen. Cornwallis, the British commander-in-chief Gen. Henry Clinton now had nearly 30,000 soldiers as a garrison for the city. Moreover, the French fleet never showed up, having gone to the South to besiege Savannah and then, failing that, back to France. So a disappointed Washington with his army went into winter quarters in the Hudson Highlands north of the city and in New Jersey. It was a long, hard winter. In January, a surprise attack by soldiers riding on sleighs over the snow was mounted against the British on Staten Island, but that amounted to nothing much.

Cornwallis

Clinton

Gen. Clinton's strategy to quell the rebellion, after the failure of the strategy of his predecessor, Maj. Gen. Howe, to divide New England from the rest of the colonies along the Hudson River Valley and Lake Champlain, was to focus militarily on the deep southern colonies where there were numerous Loyalists who he felt could be rallied. Thus, starting in December, leaving a Hessian general in charge of New York City and its environs, Clinton moved 8,000 troops to the south to besiege Charleston, South Carolina. In May, this city fell with the surrender of a large American garrison, one of the worst disasters for the patriots during the Revolution. In the North, the patriot hopes were at low ebb, too. Washington's Continentals at their winter quarters in Morristown, NJ were reduced to fewer than 4,000 soldiers, and they were mutinous due to being short on rations and for receiving their pay in near-worthless Continental dollars.

Howe

When the Culper Ring correspondence preserved in the archives resumes on May 8th, 1780, we find Maj. Tallmadge informing Gen. Washington that Culper Jr. (Robert Townsend) was looking to quit the perilous task of spying in the city. Townsend had tried to set up a more direct line of communications with Washington using his own nephew as a courier, but that had run into complications. The nephew, who was carrying an espionage report concealed in invisible ink between the lines of a poem, had stopped at the wrong house. Assuming that the inhabitants were Tories, he played Tory himself. But they were actually patriots who arrested him and turned him over to the Continental Army. Washington had him released, but a plausible cover story for his release had to be concocted to protect him and the other Culper Ring members from being found out. Moreover, Culper Sr. (Abraham Woodhull) himself was feeling timorous about continuing his own work as a spy in Setauket. The frequent boat traffic carrying messages across the Sound was drawing suspicions from the enemy. Culper Sr. wondered if "711" (Washington) knew of anyone else in the city who might be able to take Culper Jr.'s place, and he offered to contact that person and make a new arrangement. He also wondered if a particular person whom he suspected was already acting there as a source of information for Washington.

Washington was only able to pen a reply ten days later once the message had reached him at his Morristown headquarters: "As C---- junr, has totally declined and C---- Senr seems to wish to do it, I think the intercourse may be dropped, more especially as from our present position the intelligence is so long getting to hand that it is of no use by the time it reaches me." Yet, Washington was thinking ahead again to another possible campaign against the British in New York with the aid of the French fleet, once it reappeared. Consequently, he instructed Tallmadge to try to maintain Culper Sr. on Long Island on standby status to be reactivated if and when the need arose: "I would however have you take an opportunity of informing the Elder C---- that we may have occasion for his services again in the course of the Summer and that I shall be glad to employ him if it should become necessary and he is willing." In answering Woodhull's query about who else in the city might already be providing him with information and whom he could contact, Washington replied with a spymaster's circumspection, "I am endeavouring to open a communication with New York across Staten Island, but who are the agents in the city I do not know." (Actually, Washington knew more than he revealed.)

On June 10th, Culper Sr. responded to Washington's message. Woodhull expressed some irritation at what he perceived as Washington's lack of appreciation for his patriotic motives in performing the dangerous work of spying and at the fact that some of the money promised was still owed to him: "I am happy to find, that 711 is about to establish a more advantagious channel of Intelligence than heretofore. I perceive that the former he intimats hath bene but of little Service—Sorry we have bene at So much cost and trouble for little or no purpose—He also mentions of my backwardness to Serve. He certainly hath bene misinformed—you are sensible I have bene indefatigable. And have done it from a principal of duty rather than from any mercenary end—And as hinted heretofore if at any time, thers need you may rely on my faithfull endeavours—I perceive thers no mention made of any money to discharge the remaining debts. Which hath increased Since I Saw you." Culper expressed his keen hope that the French fleet would soon return and "retreive the sad misfortune of our Southern Garrison. Which dolefull Fate the papers inclosed doth two fully relate, to which I must you refer." Since he had been asked by Tallmadge to keep up his regular correspondence until receiving an answer from Washington about what he now wanted to do, he relayed information about various enemy troop movements including a major foray into New Jersey "to Surprise G.W."*

-----

* The latter incursion is what led to the Battle of Connecticut Farm in present-day Union, New Jersey, where stiff resistance from the New Jersey patriot militia discouraged Hessian Gen. Knyphausen from further pursuing an attempt to end the war in the North by catching and defeating the weakened Continental Army which was still in its winter quarters in Morristown.)

As the Long Island historian Morton Pennypacker observed, " A few week's suspension was sufficient to convince Headquarters that the services of the Culpers were indispensable." Washington wrote Tallmadge on July 11th to see if the espionage network could be reactivated now, at least, he hoped, in the case of the "elder" Culper in order to report on the enemy's doings on Long Island and in Brooklyn. Tallmadge did his persuasive best, and, by August, both of the Culpers were again reporting much as before which was greatly pleasing to Washington. Mindful of the pressing need for more timely information, Tallmadge sought out a faster, more direct route than going all the way to Setauket for the information from Culper Jr. to come out of Manhattan to Connecticut. However, boat patrols being run by the Loyalists on Long Island

Sound were making that difficult. Lt. Caleb Brewster, who was in charge of the boats carrying the information from Setauket to Connecticut, got into a fire-fight with Loyalists while he was waiting for Culper Sr., who had been into the city to bring to him a message. Brewster wanted Washington to provide him with additional Continental boats and men as reinforcements, and Woodhull put in a request for more compensation for the numerous horse trips having messages carried back and forth to New York from where Brewster's boat was landing in Setauket.

Some of the first intelligence that was now collected and reported by the reactivated spy ring proved very valuable to the revolutionary cause. It concerned a plan by Clinton to send forces to attack the French who had newly landed soldiers at Newport, Rhode Island. Townsend realized the importance of the information and had it rushed by a hard-riding Austin Roe to Setauket where Woodhull, in spite of being very sick with a fever, rushed it through means of Caleb Brewster across the Sound to Connecticut. A messenger was dispatched to warn the French in Rhode Island, and Washington had false evidence planted to be discovered by the enemy that a Continental attack on the British in New York was imminent. Clinton was totally fooled by the misinformation and ordered signal fires to be lit on Long Island to recall the naval expedition back to the city to assist with its defense against Washington's anticipated attack..

In mid-September, while unable to obtain a plan that Washington, who was still contemplating a coordinated attack on the city, wanted of the British fort in Brooklyn, Culper Jr. writing as "Amicus Republicae" was able to let Washington know about a rumor circulating in the city concerning a possible plan by Clinton of sending troops to Virginia in an attempt to rescue the Convention Army (Gen. Burgoyne's men who had surrendered at the Battle of Saratoga in 1777). Clinton had tried once before in 1778 to rescue them when they were in transit south across the Hudson from their earliest camp in Massachusetts. However, a new attempt did not come about.

In October 1780, news came of the shocking treason of Gen. Benedict Arnold who, after trying and failing to turn over West Point under his command to the enemy, fled in haste to British lines in the city. The spies had caught wind that something was afoot at West Point. Robert Townsend's sister, Sarah, who lived at the family homestead in Oyster Bay, had overheard a few snatches of conversation mentioning West Point among the British soldiers who were being quartered there. This was enough to raise suspicions. So when Tallmadge, who was currently stationed in Westchester County heard that a certain "John Anderson" had been taken prisoner with incriminating papers on his person and then on Arnold's orders been sent to West Point, Tallmadge convinced his superior officer to have "Anderson" brought back and interrogated.

Arnold

Benedict Arnold's defection led to fears that he might have known something about the existence of the Culper Ring and could expose the identities of its members. Tallmadge quickly reassured Culper Jr. that his identity was known only to himself and to nobody else in the Continental Army. In his next report from the city, Townsend described Arnold as being "much caressed" by the British and expressed sadness at the news of the execution by the Continentals of Maj. John Andre, the popular suave young British spymaster (and the real "John Anderson").

In spite of Woodhull's efforts to persuade him to stay put, after several of his "dear friends. . . In particular one that hath bene ever Servicable to this corespondence" had been arrested by the British, a dejected Townsend decided that it was best for himself to leave the city for a time and let matters cool. As Woodhull reported on November 12th, these developments meant that there was nobody in the city whom he could rely upon to send a rider to for information about what the British were up to. Although unable go there himself for the present, he hoped to do be able to do so before the onset of winter which might thereafter make further communications hard.

Meanwhile, Woodhull and Brewster had been providing Washington with intelligence about British and Loyalist strengths at Long Island locations and urging a military strike. In late November, this intelligence was put to use. With Gen. Washington's authorization, Maj. Tallmadge led a raiding party of dismounted Continental dragoons in eight boats across Long Island Sound. Leaving twenty of the men to guard the boats, the remaining sixty of the soldiers stealthily walked all the way to Mastic Neck on the south side of the island where on the 23rd they stormed with fixed bayonets Fort St. George, a heavily fortified manor house. The fort and its garrison consisting of Loyalist refugees from Rhode Island were taken by surprise in ten minutes. After destroying the fort and the supplies that it contained along with a ship moored in the harbor and after torching a stockpile of hay at another location meant for British use, Tallmadge and his men returned in triumph to Long Island with more than 50 prisoners in tow.

In April 1781, Tallmadge proposed making another such raid on Long Island and set out to collect the needed intelligence. Tallmadge was authorized by Washington to visit the French in Rhode Island to solicit their naval cooperation. He did that, but the French decided they were unable to provide any support. Meanwhile, in late April, Tallmadge renewed arrangements with Woodhull to stay in Setauket and provide intelligence while Townsend was to resume his reports from the city. Washington acceded to the arrangements which involved the need for more money but emphasized that "at the same time, I am engaging in behalf of the United States, a liberal reward for the services of the C——s, (—of whose fidelity & ability I entertain a high opinion) it is certainly but reasonable, from patriotism and every other principle, that their exertions should be proportionably great, to subserve essentially the interest of the Public."

Showing again how important this was to him, Washington provided specific instructions in a letter to Tallmadge about the kinds of information he wanted from the spies: "All the interior & minute arrangements of the Correspondence, I request you will settle with them as expeditiously & as advantageously as may be: and especially that you will urge, in very forcible terms, the necessity of having the communications as circumstantial frequent, & expeditious, as possible. The great objects of information you are very well acquainted with—such as, Arrivals, Embarkations, Preparations for Movements, alteration of Positions, situation of Posts, Fortifications, Garrisons, strength or weakness of each, distribution & strength of Corps, and in general every thing which can be interesting & important for us to know. Besides these, you are also sensible, there are many things, upon a smaller scale, which are necessary to be reported: and that whatever intelligence is communicated, ought to be not in general terms, but in detail, and with the greatest precision."

Woodhull resumed his reporting on April 23rd and was able to provide many details of the sort for which Washington was looking, including information he had procured from dining with a ship's officer in the city. On the other hand, although Woodhull said he hoped he could procure verbal accounts from him and "other persons of good observation" in the future, Townsend would not "on any account whatever" provide any further written reports. On May 12th, Tallmadge wrote to Washington that he was looking for another person to help out on Long Island who was located closer than Culper Sr. was to the city Culper Sr. contacted a candidate suggested by Tallmadge, but that person could only be sent to the city occasionally, not take up residence there. This new Culper Ring spy who signed his reports "S.G." was George Smith of Nissequogue, Long Island, who had been serving as a lieutenant in a Suffolk County Loyalist militia and had apparently become disaffected. Nissequogue, a village on the north shore of Long Island, was little more than five miles closer to New York City than Setauket.

By early June 1781, the Culper Ring had broken down altogether. Woodhull wrote on June 4th to Tallmadge about the prevailing repressive situation on Long Island and his own personal trepidations as a spy for the patriot cause: "We live in dayly fear of death and destruction, This added to my usual anxiety hath allmost unmaned me—I must now (as painfull as it is to me) disappoint your expectations, And out of my power to avoid if matters were ever So Secure on my part Which is the reverse. I dare not visit New York myself and those that have bene employed will serve no longer. Through fear I am fully perswaided by various circumstances and observation that have made from time to time—That if it Were in my power to continue it regular without any intervail, Should shortly be devoted to ruin, And it appears Clear to me that it would be presumption to take one Step further at present—And could not expect that protiction from Heaven that have hitherto enjoyed." Woodhull signed off: "You must acknowledge and readily conclude that have done all that I could, and Stood by you, when others have failed And have not left you in the darkest hour. But when our affairs appears as Clear as the Sun in the Heavens, And promiseth a Speedy and I hope a happy Conclusion."

In 1782, after Washington returned north from what had been a very successful campaign in Virginia (where Cornwallis had surrendered at Yorktown in October 1781, leading the British Crown to conclude that independence for the 13 colonies was now unavoidable), the Commander-in-Chief of the Continental Army reached out again to Maj. Tallmadge. Writing to Tallmadge on August 10th: Washington said, "I wish you without delay to open again, or at least to renew effectually, the channel of Intelligence through the C—s or any other Friends you can rely upon, in such a manner, as to keep me continually and precisely advised of every thing of consequence that passes within the Enemy's Lines. . . I know your correspondents, have heretofore, in general, been well informed, and that the only [great] difficulty has been in the circuitous route of communication, for which no other remedy can be applied but the greatest diligence & dispatch, let that be attended to, let me hear from you soon & often on these points, & believe me to be, With great regard & esteem."

Accordingly, Tallmadge met with "S.G." (George Smith) and had Smith convey Washington's instructions to the two Culpers. Tallmadge requested that Washington send him some money for the spies' expenses and more of the "stain" (secret ink), to the want of which he partly attributed the lack of the spies' correspondence. Tallmadge also told Washington he knew of a high-ranking Tory but one who was not "obnoxious" who was interested in providing information to the patriots, and Washington cautiously approved contacting him. Washington was convinced that in as much as they were "on the eve of some great Event, it is important that I should be furnished with as early & important information as can be possibly obtained." This person may be the pseudonymous "John Cork," a person whose identity we still don't know, to whom references as a source begin to appear in Tallmadge's correspondence with Washington.

By September 1782, information was once again flowing from the spies run by Tallmadge to Washington to help with his decision-making about what to do if and when the British prepared to evacuate the city at the coming of peace. The British army was reported to be selling their heavy baggage and officers' furniture in anticipation of leaving. However, the naval war continued with the French and the Spanish in the West Indies, and some ships and troops were sent there leaving a smaller garrison to defend New York. The spirits of the Loyalist refugees rose and fell as wildly different rumors circulated in the city. Some Loyalists had been leaving already with departing British ships in the hope of finding new lives for themselves in Canada.

Based on some of the intelligence he was receiving from his network of spies, Tallmadge urged Washington to authorize a "stroke" against the Loyalist troops of Col. Benjamin Thompson encamped at Huntington, Long Island, who were "very much off their Guard" and losing demoralized men through desertion. (Dealing a hard blow back at Thompson would redeem some of the humiliation for the sound beating he and his dragoons had administered in South Carolina in February 1782 to the patriot guerillas of the vaunted "Swamp Fox," Francis Marion.) Washington approved the plan and ordered reinforcements for Tallmadge. Yet, to Tallmadge's extreme disappointment, the punitive expedition scheduled for December 5th which was on the point of embarking from Connecticut for Long Island had to be given up when strong winds lasting for two days and nights prevented the boats from crossing the Sound. Instead his martial spirit had to be satisfied with a battle that took place with three boatloads of Loyalists who were trying to make it back to Long Island from trading and spying on the Connecticut shore. Unfortunately, Tallmadge's friend and colleague, Capt. Caleb Brewster, was severely wounded in the engagement. Hostilities between the United States and Great Britain ceased officially in April 1783 making this one of the last times that blood was shed in the American Revolution.

Maj. Tallmadge continued his service with a light infantry unit on the Connecticut shore trying to check "the frequent & growing Intercourse with Long Island" and collecting information to pass upward. Maj. Tallmadge's last communication of substance to Gen. Washington was dated August 16, 1783. Tallmadge reminded Washington that a final monetary accounting was due to Culper and others for "secret Services" and provided Washington with the details. He ended his letter, with victory finally now in sight, giving his heart-felt thanks for their relationship:

> "Should I not have an oppprtunity [sic] to pay my personal respects to Your Excellency before You retire from the Army, give me leave at this Time, with the warmest Gratitude, to assure Your Excellency that I shall ever entertain a lively sense of the many marks of attention which I have recd from Your Excellency's hands. Whatever may have been the result, it gives me great pleasure to reflect, that during my Service in the Army, it has ever been my highest ambition to merit Your Excellency's Approbation. In the Calm retirements of domestic life, may You continue to enjoy health; and may you find increasing Satisfaction from the reflexion of having Conducted the Arms of America thro' a War so peculiarly distressing to the Obtainment of an honorable Peace; and of having been the Instrument, under God, in obtaining the freedom & Independence of this Country. Advice, my Dear General; and in every Situation of Life I pray you to believe that my best wishes will attend You, & that I shall Continue to be, as I am at this time,

with every Sentiment of Respect and Esteem, Your Excellency's most Obedt &
very Hble Servt."

Washington replied on September 11th that, with a little further documentation from
Tallmadge, he would try to cover whatever money was outstanding although it would be "no
very easy matter" because the states, he rued, cared little for past services and the means to
reward them. (Under the Articles of Confederation, tax money for the use of the U.S.
government had to be raised by the states. Washington may have been thinking here about what
had happened in March in the so-called "Newburgh Conspiracy" when officers in the
Continental Army threatened to mutiny over arrears in pay and the lack of funding for a
promised pension.) At the same time, although Washington thanked Tallmadge for the kind
words expressed in his letter and said he felt that to no other officer in the army was he more
indebted than to Tallmadge for his happy reflections in the future, his remarks about the service
of the Culper spies were surprisingly critical and niggardly rather than generous and appreciative
of their contributions:

> "I have no doubt, because I suppose S:C: to be an honest Man, that the Monies
> charged in his Acct have been expended, & therefore should be paid; but the
> Services which were rendered by him (however well meant) was by no means
> adequate to these Expenditures—My Complaints on this head, before I knew the
> amount of his charges, you may remember were frequent; and but for the request
> of Count de Rochambeau, who told me that he had put money into your hands, &
> would continue to furnish you with more for the purpose of obtaining intelligence
> through this Channel I should have discontinued the Services of S.C. long before
> a cessation of hostilities took place, because his communications were never
> frequent, and always tedious in getting to hand."

The last British troops evacuated from New York on November 25, 1783, and a select corp of
the Continental Army soldiers marched in triumph into the city later the same day to wildly
cheering crowds. As peace seemed certain and looking ahead to when the British finally left,
Tallmadge in a letter to Washington in March 31, 1783 had requested that he and his detachment
be among the first allowed to enter the city so that he could protect from mistreatment as Tories
"certain Characters in New York, who have served us very essentially, & who may otherwise be
treated amiss — It is a favor which they will by all means expect, & some of them will not wish
to have the nature of thier services divulged." Washington concurred about the "propriety in
your going early into Town whenever the communication shall be opened" with or without
Tallmadge's detachment depending on the circumstances.

In his memoir, Tallmadge describes how he had subsequently entered the city under a flag of
truce where, after dining with the British Commander-in-Chief, Gen. Guy Carlton. and other
British officers, he "saw and secured all who had been friendly to us through the war, and
especially our emissaries, so that not one instance occurred of any abuse, after we took

possession of the city, where protection was given or engaged." Tallmadge was likely most concerned about the fate of his deepest source, the newspaper editor James Rivington, who, to all outward appearances, had been a "notorious Tory" and thus, since he had not gone into exile with other Loyalists might have been mobbed by angry patriots for his pro-British journalism. As soon as the patriot troops entered the city, Rivington was protected by the posting of a guard. A post-revolutionary story, perhaps apocryphal, is that Washington himself visited Rivington to express his deep appreciation and to give him a reward in the form of a bag of gold coins.

Chapter 4: After the War

Major Benjamin Tallmadge was among those officers who were present on December 4, 1783 when Washington bid his wartime comrades adieu at a tavern in New York City to return to his home at Mt. Vernon in Virginia. Tallmadge then paid a visit to his own hometown of Brookhaven on Long Island, from which he had been banished for seven years during the war and was there reunited with and was feted by his family and old friends. In the spring of 1784, Tallmadge married the daughter of a wealthy Long Island landowner William Floyd, a signer of the "Declaration of Independence," and settled as a merchant and banker in Litchfield, Connecticut. Before the war was over, Tallmadge had been one of the founders of the Society of the Cincinnati, an hereditary order of former Continental Army and Navy officers. He served as the first treasurer and later president of the Connecticut chapter before it was dissolved because of popular opposition to its hereditary nature. From 1801 to 1817, Tallmadge represented his district as a Federalist in the U.S. Congress. He died at the age of 81 in 1835.

Captain Caleb Brewster following the end of the war married a woman from Fairfield, Connecticut and together they raised a large family. He farmed and worked as a blacksmith in Fairfield until 1793 when he took a job with the United States Revenue-Marine that had been established by Congress for the armed enforcement of customs laws for the new nation. Brewster commanded a revenue cutter during the War of 1812. He died in 1827 at the age of 80.

Abraham Woodhull (Samuel Culper Sr.) remained in Setauket after the war where he ended his bachelor existence by marrying a cousin and having three children. He served as a Suffolk County magistrate from 1799 to 1810. He freed his slaves and died in 1826 at the age of 75. His tombstone mentions nothing of his Revolutionary War service as a spy, but the DAR added a plaque detailing it in 1936. According to his surviving account book, the remaining amount that the nation owed him as expenses for his espionage services was finally paid to him in 1790.

Anna Strong lived out the rest of her life in Setauket with her patriot husband, Selah Strong, who had spent part of the war incarcerated on a British prison ship. They had nine children, and it is from a family tradition passed down generation to generation that we hear about Anna's role in using her laundry as signal flags for the Culper Ring. She died in 1812 at the age of 72.

Robert Townsend (Samuel Culper Jr.) moved following the war, after his import business in New York City failed, back to where he was from originally in Oyster Bay, Long Island. He never married, although he seems to have sired an illegitimate son with his housekeeper. He died in 1838 at the age of 84. Today, his former home, Raynham Hall, is a town museum.

James Rivington briefly published a reinvented newspaper without the "Royal" in its title after the British and Loyalists left New York but was shutdown after twelve issues by patriot leaders whom he had antagonized. He spent the rest of his life in poverty and died at age 78 in 1802.

Austin Roe, the chief courier for the Culper Ring, operated a tavern in East Setauket, where George Washington overnighted on a tour of Long Island in 1790. There is no evidence that Washington knew or was told the story about who he was staying with. Roe died in 1830 at the age of 81. A newly-discovered letter shows that several other Roes were involved in the spying.

The identity and fate of another member of the Culper Ring, known only by her numerical designation, "355," thought to be a New York City society woman, remains still to be discovered.

Two other patriot spies in New York City who occasionally worked for Washington on their own and sometimes conveyed information via the Culper Ring need to be acknowledged. They were the brothers Hercules and Hugh Mulligan. Hercules, a former member of the New York City Sons of Liberty and Committee of Correspondence, was in a excellent position to collect information in his occupation as a tailor serving the sartorial needs of the British officer corps. Hugh had economic ties with the British military through his import-export business. Washington's aide, Alexander Hamilton, who had boarded with the Mulligan household as a student at King's College (Columbia) before the war, may have recommended their services. Based on suspicions provided the British by Matthew Arnold, Hercules Mulligan was arrested and held for some months in prison, but he was ultimately released. Hercules's black slave, Cato, was sometimes used as a courier to carry information outside of the British lines. Washington showed his appreciation for Hercules Mulligan's help by breakfasting with him after the British evacuated.

Whether out of personal modesty or because espionage was considered a less-than-noble occupation than soldiering or for some other reasons, the members of the Culper Ring said little or nothing during their own lifetimes about their clandestine activities in support of the patriot cause. The identity of Robert Townsend as Samuel Culper Jr. was not uncovered until the 1930's when the local Long Island historian, Morton Pennypacker, was asked to look at a collection of papers and ledgers belonging to Townsend found in Oyster Bay. In a brilliant bit of historical detective work, Pennypacker with the help of a graphologist was able to match the handwriting in those documents with that in Culper, Jr.'s letters to Washington. Pennypacker wrote up his findings in a book, *George Washington's Spies on Long Island and in New York*, that was published in 1939 and which included much of the correspondence involving the Culper Ring.

Because he escaped retribution for his newspaper's rabidly pro-British stance and its libels against patriot leaders, rumors circulated almost immediately at the war's end about James Rivington's possible role serving as a spy for George Washington. While there is no "smoking gun," there is good circumstantial evidence that Rivington, given the designation "726" in Tallmadge's code book, was a member of the Culper Ring (and not just another one of the British enemy such as Gen. Clinton also designated with a number). As Catherine Snell Cray pointed out in her 1959 article, "The Tory and the Spy: The Double Life of James Rivington," for the prestigious *William & Mary Quarterly*, Rivington had both the opportunity with his newspaper and the popular coffeehouse he ran (co-owned with Culper Jr., Robert Townsend) and the motive (growing financial troubles) to conduct espionage. Moreover, one of Washington's lieutenants, Col. Allan McLane, reported in his recollections that he had obtained a copy of the British naval code book from Rivington and turned it over for the French to use in 1781 prior to the victory at Yorktown.

It is possible that more information will be found by historians about the Culper Ring spies, possibly in British archives from the Revolutionary War that have not yet been fully explored.

Chapter 5: How Important was the Culper Ring?

The authors of a recent popular book on the Culper Ring subtitled their book *The Spy Ring That Saved the American Revolution*. This kind of hyperbole may be a good way to market one's book, but how accurate is it? At the very least, we can say that it stands at odds with Washington's own less-than-glowing assessment of the service provided by the spies at the end of the war and his stated reluctance to pay the outstanding balance owed them for their expenses.

The argument by Brian Kilmeade and Don Yaeger that the Culper Ring "saved" the Revolution is based on the report by Continental officer Allan McLane that the British naval codebook was obtained by him from Rivington and then passed on to the French admiral de Grasse, who, they claim, used the vital information to help defeat the fleet of British admiral Graves off the Virginia Capes on September 5, 1781 thus preventing rescue and sealing the fate of Cornwallis at Yorktown, the deciding battle of the war for independence. However, we do not know for sure that de Grasse actually received the codebook in time to do that or, if so, made use of it. In any case, De Grasse outnumbered Graves in terms of ships and guns, and the British admiral made a possibly calamitous mistake in issuing conflicting signals. So one could certainly argue that the French would have won regardless of whether their admiral had the British codebook in hand.

De Grasse

Graves

Washington's plan, before removing the bulk of his army accompanied by the French army to Virginia, had been to attack the British in New York and liberate the occupied city. If Cornwallis had not elected to march northward to Virginia where he put himself into a vulnerable position and if Washington had not decided seize that golden military opportunity being presented, then history might have gone quite differently. In that case, the information provided by the Culper Ring from inside British lines in New York might have made a major difference in enabling a successful attack. The information provided by the Culper Ring did help Washington to stay on top of British army and naval strength and their coming and goings in and around New York City but, as things turned out, seems to have contributed only some to the eventual patriot victory.

A former employee of the Central Intelligence Agency, Kenneth A. Daigler, has written a book on espionage during the American Revolution. With his insider knowledge of spycraft, Daigler, in his chapter "American Intelligence Activities Reach Maturity", gives significant credit to the Culper Ring agents and their handler for developing professional methods of conveying information and for keeping their identities and activities secret with plausible cover stories. Daigler identifies three instances in which intelligence gathered by the Culper Ring proved to be of significant importance: First, in July 1779, a report from Townsend exposed the identity of a Tory agent posing as a patriot who was providing information to the Loyalist mayor of New York, David Mathews. Second, in November 1779, Townsend passed on the information that the British had acquired the matching kind of paper needed to counterfeit Continental currency and thus devalue it, enabling Congress to recall all its currency and thwart the plan. Third, a report from Townsend in July 1780 warned Washington that Clinton was planning to dispatch a force to attack the newly-arrived French force at Newport, Rhode Island before they could get sufficiently organized (Clinton had learned of the French plans from the traitorous Benedict Arnold). As we have seen, Washington skillfully used that information to plant misinformation that he was going to attack New York City, thus causing Clinton to recall his troops to the city.

A fourth instance may be added when the Culper Ring certainly aided the eventual success of the American Revolution. In early March 1781, information from Hercules Mulligan was passed on by the Ring that the British planned to try to capture Washington while he was *en route* to meet with French general Rochambeau, and Washington was able to alter his route. Given Washington's importance to the cause, perhaps it can be argued that this did save the Revolution.

The Culper Ring has been featured in American literature and popular culture. The first best-selling American novel was James Fenimore Cooper's *The Spy: A Tale of the Neutral Ground* (1821). Although set in Westchester County, NY, its historical inspiration may have been the Culper Ring, and the novel's main protagonist, Harvey Birch, a combination of the two Culpers. It may or may not be significant that Cooper's wife was a cousin of Benjamin Tallmadge's wife.

Recently, the Culper Ring was gotten more attention from historians and certainly much more from the general public because of an AMC cable TV show, *Turn: Washington's Spies*, now with a third season in production. Although a well-crafted drama, the plots take some liberties with the historical record and thus can be misleading. For instance, the spies begin their work in 1776 rather than in 1778, and the town of Setauket is occupied by British redcoats rather than green-uniformed Loyalists. Also, although it adds some spice to the plot, without any historical documentation and in spite of their actual differences in age (she's older by 10 years), Abraham Woodhull (played by Jamie Bell) and Anna Strong (played by Heather Lind) are portrayed as contemporaries who carry on a torrid secret love affair. So enjoy watching the show but *caveat emptor*. A blog to critique the show and provide historically-accurate information about the Culpers has been created by historians: "Turn to a Historian" https://spycurious.wordpress.com/

Online Resources

Other Revolutionary War titles by Charles River Editors

Other titles about the Culper Ring on Amazon

Other titles about Revolutionary War spies on Amazon

Bibliography

Allen, Thomas B., and Cheryl Harness. *George Washington, Spymaster: How the Americans Outspied the British and Won the Revolutionary War.* Washington D.C.: National Geographic Books, 2007.

Andrlik, Todd. "James Rivington: King's Printer and American Spy?" *Journal of the American Revolution,* March 3, 2014. http://allthingsliberty.com/2014/03/james-rivington-kings-printer-patriot-spy/.

Crary, Catherine Snell. "The Tory and the Spy: The Double Life of James Rivington." *The William and Mary Quarterly: A Magazine of Early American History,* 1959, 61–72.

Daigler, Kenneth A. Spies, *Patriots, and Traitors: American Intelligence in the Revolutionary War.* Washington D.C.: Georgetown University Press, 2014.

"Founders Online: Correspondence and Other Writings of Six Major Shapers of the United States." National Archives, n.d. http://founders.archives.gov/.

Kilmeade, Brian, and Don Yaeger. *George Washington's Secret Six: The Spy Ring That Saved the American Revolution.* New York: Sentinel, 2013.

Pennypacker, Morton. *General Washington's Spies on Long Island and in New York.* Brooklyn, N.Y: The Long Island Historical Society, 1939.

Schellhammer, Michael. "Abraham Woodhull: The Spy Named Samuel Culper." *Journal of the American Revolution,* May 19, 2014. http://allthingsliberty.com/2014/05/abraham-woodhull-the-spy-named-samuel-culper/.

Tallmadge, Benjamin. *Memoir of Col. Benjamin Tallmadge.* New York: Thomas Holman, 1858.

Thompson, Benjamin F. *History of Long Island; Containing an Account of the Discovery and Settlement; with Other Important and Interesting Matters to the Present Time.* New York: E.

French, 1839.

Ward, Christopher L.. *The War of the Revolution*. Edited by John Richard Alden. 2 vols. New York: Macmillan Company, 1952.

Made in the USA
Middletown, DE
30 October 2016